Sisters of the Protectress

by

darlene st. georges and alexandra fidyk

Finishing Line Press
Georgetown, Kentucky

Sisters of the Protectress—
A Creation Story

Copyright © 2024 by darlene st. georges and alexandra fidyk
ISBN 979-8-88838-633-0 First Edition
All rights reserved under International and Pan-American Copyright Conventions. No part of this book may be reproduced in any manner whatsoever without written permission from the publisher, except in the case of brief quotations embodied in critical articles and reviews.

Publisher: Leah Huete de Maines
Editor: Christen Kincaid
Cover Art & Design: "Sisters of the Protectress" by darlene st. georges
Content Art & Design: Digital visual rendering of (free) stock images become creative artworks to interweave poetically with the written text by darlene st. georges
Author Photos: darlene st. georges and Diane Tordjman

Order online: www.finishinglinepress.com
  also available on amazon.com

Author inquiries and mail orders:
Finishing Line Press
PO Box 1626
Georgetown, Kentucky 40324
USA

Contents

1	unearth tongues from dream
2	Crow Comes Back Moon
4	in the silence
5	We rise
8	in caves and wombs
9	appearing and disappearing
10	ink-dressed Mother of Covid
11	blood lines
12	Bear Woman
13	Crow Mother
14	Good Mother
15	Land and Sky
16	telling the untellable
17	facing west
18	on gravel stones
19	I dreamt
20	I remember
21	I could hear
22	honing the ear
23	Grandmother
24	catch me
25	Winged-Onyx Sister
27	the Ancestors are calling
28	Grandmother's songs
29	stitched under my wing
30	verses teach us
31	She rides
32	time to feel
34	I belong to you
35	We are related
36	fur and feather
37	unearthing tongues between worlds

To the places where we dream—

to unearth tongues from dream, blood memory, and lifelines
fragmented stories told at immeasurable distances
demand attention

> From our very first breath, we are in relationship. With that indrawn draft of air, we become joined to everything that ever was, is and ever will be.
> —Richard Wagamese, *Embers: One Ojibway's Meditations*, 2016, p. 44

We amplify the languages of Bear Woman and Crow Mother in this tale of tongues to honour the movements of these Sisters in two worlds that co-emerge. Bear and Crow time shift through concentric circling, layering season and place, dream and memory to generate a creation story that calls upon ancestral relations of Land, Sky, Water, and Cosmos. This telling begins with "Crow Comes Back Moon," the Northern Algonquin term for the Worm Moon, which occurred in March 2021 (Almanac, 2021). From the depth of the dark Earth womb, we cross the celestial veil to ignite the imaginative and mythological realms. We engage in the paradox of the inner and outer, upper and lower worlds, real and imaginal.

We use creation-centred métissage, amplification, circumambulation, and poiesis to interweave narratives. "Creation-centred métissage" (St. Georges, 2024) is situated in a creative aesthetic and an ethos of métissage. It is an inspirited and critically fluid storying praxis generated within a realm of agency held in a living cosmos. It is an inward-outward journeying that attends to our living spectres—our stories and our ancestral memories that reside in the deep cavities of our being. It explores connections between inner and outer realms of experience, as a way to expand knowledge relationally (St. Georges, 2024). To amplify the image, we looked for its associations and meanings through a slow and thoughtful collection of parallels. This act of enlargement asks us to attend somatically and tease apart the "clustering attraction of the symbol" (von Franz, 1970, p. 71). For us, the term image arises from poetic usage, "it does not arrive from thought nor is it the outcome of perception. Images arrive already as givens of life" (Fidyk, 2010, p. 2). "Every psychic process is an image and an 'imagining'" (Jung, CW11, para. 889), and these images are "as real as you—as a psychic entity—are real" (CW14, para. 753). "Images are spontaneous, primordial, always arising" (Fidyk, 2010, p. 2); Image is the soul presenting itself. Amplifying an image constellates a field with emotional, sensorial, and sensuous effects that then beckons other images, memories, symbols, and associations. Here both listener and teller become enveloped in the very thing itself. This envelopment, like a cocoon, is the "active ingredient" (von Franz, 1970, p. 71) that empowers us to undergo transformation, which, in turn, affects the mood and ethos of place. Circumambulation, like spinning and weaving, creates a rhythmic movement of rounding a node, bringing each previous parallel forward. It permits us to reflect on the image from different points of view. This process arouses emotional and feeling material that directs us—a following of sorts. Circumambulation differs from egocentric linking, which moves linearly and operates in isolation, evading the aliveness and agency—the fullness—of the image (Fidyk & St. Georges, 2022; St. Georges & Fidyk, 2023).

As artists, we are propelled to explore what is more about being and living. To do so, we enter into the lives of Bear and Crow through thick poetic description and imaginal dialogues. They encounter one another in the splendour of Alberta grasslands under the acute angle of spring sun. Bear and Crow come into relation through body–to–body echoing. Fallow soil has been priming for creative renewal where earthworms rise to the surface after their hibernation. Withstanding her dormant period, Bear emerges from her slumber. Shaking off her slowed breath and quieted heart, she readies to make the journey to the river for her first feeding. Migratory birds attuned to their morphic resonances of flight have chosen local waters to begin their nesting and mating rituals. Mated pairs of crows have come back with family members from migration. Crow returns to reclaim her territory in sacred backyard spaces.

in the silence

    under the pillar of my tongue
        in caves and wombs

        between   time and space   sleep
                  and wake

            a movement inward

spilling out Earth's Meditations amidst the drum
        in motion and place within the pluriverse
    We rise
               to the beat of our relations   in
                    reciprocity
                    reverence
                    renewal

calling the Ancestors—

Bear Woman

exists

in the deep silence of things
where you dream yourself alive

.

.

.

.

.

[pouring out vision]

She
remembered intensely—ached it, lived it, learned it
in the silence: in caves and wombs

finding her way
walking, running, drinking from rivers
tasting new rains and shoots
yawning, stretching

leaning into heart
leaning into vulnerability
liberating her body and spirit
resetting consciousness to day light
among hues of green grasses
and imperceptible rhythms
that ignite imaginaries

[lavishing]

appearing and disappearing
in a flux of exquisite voices

Crow Mother
ink-dressed
Mother of Covid
hoarse caws
from Her keen-eye perch

returns from winter's communal roost
She readies Her fallow form
for new life

a messenger between worlds
She warns of Death
signaling its ever-presence

appearing and disappearing
in a flux of exquisite voices

one among a murder
anything but common

blood lines tap root

interwoven generations
evanescent waves of knowing
that run long and deep, rhizomatic
primed for Death Water

Bear Woman walks through
the maze of skeptics
with the passing equinox
season-by-season
weathering storms
unearthing seeds
with sun-drenched jaws

She moves with easterly winds
dances circles
squeezes dreams

centred in solitude

existing as She exists—

Crow Mother
circles spruce peaks
weaving the past into now
in constant chorus
She inter-winds our worlds

Her beak tears the flesh of new spring

retrieving silver foil
and plastic caps
to line Her twig crown
Scavenger Architect

[undercurrents]

Crow Mother
Good Mother

feeds Her squalling chicks
succulent morsels of yolk abundance
transferred wisdom of the genus
nourishes tentative hearts
in their webbed crown of black poplar

freshwater backyard basins
adorned with ligaments, claws, and feathers
reddened fragments of Sparrow

become Death Water offering

[moon pulled permeable spaces]

                                                Bear Woman

                                       traverses Land and Sky
                                                    lumbering
                                                    flatfooted
                                              aromatic tailings
                                     link Her water-bound descent
                                                with our imaginary

                                             golden honey eggs
                                                 primed for life
                                           She rips from its belly

                                                    sanctuary

                        carcasses strewn across sun-bleached rocks
                                           stolen salmon treasures

                        [raw and bursting parabola]

Giving testimony births a new story—telling the untellable.

I awoke to the middle road
a long, long dusty road and I am facing west

I believe I've been here before, but I can't be sure. I've been travelling for so long now and feel weary. I've been searching for the river, the one lined with red willow, low brushes, and thick black poplars, where Crow lives. Could I have taken a wrong turn somehow? It's dry here; dust and stones, wide skies, and grasses, and it reeks of Death. Even standing on my hinds, squinting long and hard, I can't seem to see what I'm looking for.

I'll walk until I can see the constellations . . .

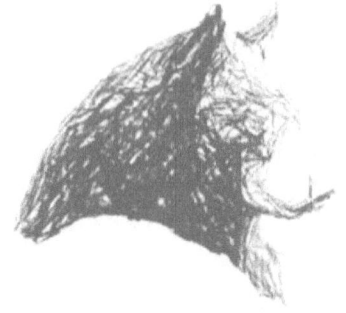

[equatorial return]

hopping on the gravel stones
I am disrupted by the arrival of Bear
I hear Her snorts, long snout collecting scent

chasing the furthest daydream, I came
to drink at that abundant well
where saps and all secretions
gather to soak the world's roots

You see through all
my thoughts.

Butterfly rests
on a domed fungus. Her wings
folding, unfolding, fan
rich musk which hints all growth
in subterranean gardens

Bearing Witness—

I dreamt

I could fly above the trees
I was frolicking with winds
dipping and soaring across seas
shouting out to my friends below
but they couldn't hear me or see me

                                                I was alone on this journey—

I remember

after moments of doubt

I could hear

                        a kaleidoscope of
                           bone songs
                            rooted in
            the cusp of low flying birds

                 remnants of knowledge
                   lodged in mountains

                    aspects of wisdom
                     woven in stories
            swaddled throughout time

[field of memory]

after moments of doubt

I remember

I dreamt

I could hear

the stories

the ones that cross time and space
the ones that can help us navigate
our way through . . .

in the memory of wind
in the tender rhythms
in the soundings of Earth
in the echoes
in the resonances
found in fertile hearts of life—
its roots and vertices
its breath

in the songs of unfettered beings
that shift realities in jade forests
and sky dancers—
primordial beings
who exist within frequencies
that draw out our view

[beyond our own horizon]

not everything that goes
leaves a trail

wind of flight
of memory
of unfamiliar sounds
different alphabets

honing   all honing the ear

                                        Do you hear?

Grandmother was a Storyteller. I remember Her telling. Held in Her arms, I hear Her voice gather in the rhythm of late spring, the night chorus of Frog, thick croaking, promising continuance. Her melodic notes ride the warm breeze curling round the slender red willows.

the ear of my heart attunes
to the teachings of place
ancient grasslands, mountains, hoodoos

groves of sister aspen
tender shoots seeking sweet rain
binding earth, air and fire
into my prayers for renewal

Her voice pulses into
cellular depths of my body
flesh of Her dark imagination

                    I still feel the wonder of the treed world . . .

          stories lost

        We need more Storytellers—

I know She wants to catch me
not eat me but
to change places. She wants to touch
my coal-drenched form, to lose Her fur and teeth
to grow feathers, to flee with the others
hot musty breath of
Her muzzle beating
on the back of my neck.

Are We all trying to outrun
the other? avoid inevitable capture—

I throw forth as She leaps to catch a wing

fleeting unsurfaced borders
wide-eyed
I see myself in Crow
Winged-Onyx Sister

Her exquisite wings refracting light
meanwhile I am here
crushed by gravity
shuttling between breaths
crawling across fragments of

as the winds blow through me

downwind
downwind
downwind
downwind
downwind

the Ancestors are calling—

Grandmother taught us the same songs—they begin with the time when there is only Spider Woman. She spun two threads and where they crossed, She sat singing. Her singing held everything together.

                                                                Do you hear her Sister Bear?

I strain for Her voice
always there in the background
like the turning of Mother Earth.

I recall verses of songs I sang with Grandmother
stitched under my wing

echoing
echoing
echoing

in patterns around us
hauntings now—
felt as longings, lost moorings and up-rootings

Her verses teach us that life is an exchange. We breathe in and we breathe out. All things wax and wane, rounding through place and time—

even the winds and clouds and the
crowns of old spruce participate

see the patterns they weave
binding soil and sky

We are enfolded, entwined into Her singing
beginning long before our birthing
and ringing onward after our death.

> She gifts
> mystery of the threshold
> where promise lies in the turning
> turning

It is said that She rides the hedgerows at twilight on a pale horse
accompanied by Crow

always Crow

Foreteller
Lawmaker
Truth-keeper

I awoke to the setting sun—
bursts of magenta and tangerine

what a breathtaking sight—

a time to feel

earth
sky
land

[constellations]

—Great [She] Bear

I believe I belong to you

like hues of light and fragile moments
sharing the limits of one another in dark poplar forests
grasslands
and subterranean gardens—

[pulsating frequencies]

We are related

                                                            entwined
                                                            interwoven

                          like a spring amulet

                            refracting light
                          through one breath
                              and then
                              another

Sisters of the Protectress
hybridity of fur and feather

unearthing tongues between worlds

Acknowledgments

Grateful acknowledgments to the following anthology and collections where some of the poems in this book have been published or will soon appear:

Voices Unbound: Poems of the Eighth International Symposium on Poetic Inquiry (2023)—

alexandra fidyk: "Crow Mother Meets Bear Woman," "We are Related," and "Grandmother's Songs";

darlene st. georges: "To Unearth Tongues," "Facing West," and "Bear Woman Meets Crow Mother."

Arts Creation: A Curriculum of Relationality, Resurgence, and Renewal (2023)—
darlene st. georges: "in caves and wombs."

References

Almanac Publishing Co. (2021). Astronomy. *Farmers' almanac.* https://www.farmersalmanac.com/full-moon-dates-and-times

Jung, C. G. (1958/1989). Psychology and religion: West and east. (Trans. R. F. C. Hull). In H. Read, M. Fordham, G. Adler, & W. McGuire (Eds.), *Bollingen series collected works 11*. Princeton University Press.

Jung, C. G. (1963/1989). Mysterium coniunctionis: An inquiry into the separation and synthesis of psychic opposites in alchemy. (Trans. R. F. C. Hull). In H. Read, M. Fordham, G. Adler, & W. McGuire (Eds.), *Bollingen series collected works 14*. Princeton University Press.

Fidyk, A. (2010). Hermaphrodite as healing image: Connecting a mythic imagination to education. *Jungian Journal of Scholarly Studies, 6*(2), 1-32. http://jungiansociety.org/images/e-journal/Volume-6/Fidyk-2010.pdf

Fidyk, A., & St. Georges, D. (2022). The gifting of Feather: Kaleidoscopic visioning to reanimate learning. In E. Lyle (Ed.), *Re/centering lives and lived experience in education* (pp. 13-41). Brill.

St. Georges, D., & Fidyk, A. (2023). Red Thread dancing|Feather dreaming. In E. Lyle, J. Yeon Ryu, & C. Snowber (Eds.), *Qualitative Inquiry, 30*(2), 226-256. https://doi.org/10.1177/10778004231176102

St. Georges, D. (2024). Embodied landscapes: A creation-centred métissage of self-in relation. In J. Markides, & D. St. Georges (Eds.), *Arts creation: A curriculum of relationality, resurgence, and renewal* (pp. 337-365). DIO Press.

Von Franz, M.-L. (1970). *The interpretation of fairy tales.* Revised edition. Shambhala.

Wagamese, R. (2016). *Embers: One Ojibway's meditations.* Douglas & McIntyre.

darlene st. georges, PhD. is a creation-centred artist|scholar. She is associate professor of art education at the University of Lethbridge, Alberta, Canada. Her theoretical and practice-based research is rooted in emergent and generative knowledge and knowing that honours the inward and creative ways being—living literacies expressed through aesthetic translations of voice, breath, body, and spirit. Her poetry has been published in International *Journal of Art and Design Education* 38(3), *Art/Research International: A Transdisciplinary Journal* V7(1), *Qualitative Studies, International Journal of Fear Studies, Canadian Review of Art Education* (45)1, *Artizien: Arts and Teaching Journal* (V5) & (V7), *Journal of the Canadian Association for Curriculum Studies* (14)1, *Journal of Jungian Scholarly Studies, and Poetic Inquiry for Synchrony & Love: A New Order of Gravity* (forthcoming). Her artwork has been published as covers for several journals and books such as: *Art|Research International: A transdisciplinary Journal* V7(2), *Canadian Review of Art Education* (45)1, *Artizien: Arts and Teaching Journal* V5(1), *A Métissage of Inspiration/Imagination/Interconnections* (Canadian Curriculum Studies), *Arts Creation: A Curriculum of Relationality, Resurgence and Renewal* (DIO Press), *Poetic Inquiry: Enchantment of Place* (Vernon Press), *Poetic Inquiry* She has a self-published book *"From Left to Right"* (Magcloud). Darlene is co-editor of Artizein: Arts & Teaching Journal. Contact: darlene.stgeorges@ uleth.ca See: GAIA Studio www.darlenestgeorges.com

alexandra fidyk, PhD, is an award-winning teacher-educator and transdisciplinary scholar. As professor, she serves in the Faculty of Education, University of Alberta, Canada, where she teaches curriculum studies, advanced research, analytical psychology, trauma studies, and teacher education. Recently launched, she designed and leads an Educational Studies graduate certificate in Trauma-Sensitive Practice. A philosopher, poet, and somatic psychotherapist (trauma-specialized), she engages with teachers, youth, and health-care professionals on issues of love, suffering, home, and wellbeing using somatic, relational, poetic and creative-centred processes. She is registered and certified as a Jungian Psychotherapist; Integrated Body Psychotherapist; Somatic Experiencing Practitioner; Expressive Arts Therapist; Family Systems & Inherited Family Trauma Facilitator; and Sandplay Therapy trainee. Her poetry has been published in the following journals: *Language & Literacy, Jung Journal, Spring: A Journal of Archetype and Culture, Quadrant, ARAS Connections: Image & Archetype, Poiesis, How Can I Keep From Singing?* and *These Small Hours*. Other publications include: *Poetic Inquiry for Synchrony & Love: A New Order of Gravity* (forthcoming); *Reclaiming the Fire: Archetypal Reflectivity in Three Voices* (2019); *Poetic Inquiry: Enchantment of Place* (2017); *Democratizing Educational Experience: Envisioning, Embodying, Enacting* (2008). Contact: fidyk@ualberta.ca See: https://apps.ualberta.ca/directory/person/fidyk

www.ingramcontent.com/pod-product-compliance
Lightning Source LLC
Chambersburg PA
CBHW020343170426
43200CB00006B/493